Woke Up This Morning

Woke Up This Morning
Brian Docherty

Published 2012 by
Smokestack Books
PO Box 408, Middlesbrough TS5 6WA
e-mail: info@smokestack-books.co.uk
www.smokestack-books.co.uk

Woke Up This Morning
Brian Docherty
Copyright 2012, by Brian Docherty
Cover image: Irma Irsara, *L'acqua dialoga coi sassi*
Author photo: ArmsLength Images

Printed by
EPW Print & Design Ltd

ISBN 978-0-9571722-2-7

Smokestack Books is
represented by Inpress Ltd
www.inpressbooks.co.uk

for Rosemary

Acknowledgements are due to the editors of the following magazines and anthologies:

Acumen, The Affectionate Punch, Brando's Hat, Brittle Star, Fire, Dress of Nettles (Ragged Raven Press, 2004), *Envoi, Gutter, The Interpreter's House, Iota, Life, Death, Sex & Chocolate* (New Gallery Books, 2002), *London Grip, Loose Cannon, Magma, Poetry Ealing, Poetry News, Poetry Salzburg, Poetry Scotland, Poetry Street N16, Quattrocento, The Reater, The Rialto, The Slab, Southfields, Stop Me And Buy One* (Word for Word, Wood Green 2005), *The World is Made of Glass* (Ragged Raven Press, 2010).

'Naughty Boy' was a runner-up in the Ilkley Literature Festival Poetry Competition 1999; 'Mr Quercus Speaks His Mind' won the Muswell Hill & Fortis Green Poetry Competition 2002; 'The "if" in California' was highly commended in the Poetry Plus 7 Competition 2002; 'In My Dreams' was a runner-up in the Yorkshire Open Poetry Competition 2002; 'Hostage to Fortune' won 3rd Prize in the Split The Lark Poetry Competition 2003; 'Living in the Light' was a runner-up in the Ragged Raven Press Poetry Competition 2003; Doing Time in the Movies' was a runner-up in the Ottakar's/Faber Poetry Competition 2003; 'Lost At Sea' was a runner-up in the Ottakar's/Faber Poetry Competition 2004; 'Rodin's *Left Hand* was commended in the Pitshanger Poetry Competition 2007.

Contents

- 11 Alphabet
- 12 Kraut
- 13 Weather Reports
- 14 Born to be Wild
- 15 The Reddest Shoes
- 16 Buttons
- 17 Cloths from Rajasthan
- 18 Coming Back to Clear Up
- 19 Reincarnation
- 20 Naughty Boy
- 21 Holiday Joke
- 22 Thinking Your Way Round Clichés
- 23 Jacob and the Angel
- 24 All We Are Saying
- 25 Attachments
- 26 Manchester's Big Mistake
- 27 Refugee Status
- 28 Exhibit
- 29 In My Dreams
- 30 Rodin's *Left Hand*
- 31 The Artist's Mother as Simple Catholic Peasant
- 32 Art Gallery Weather
- 33 Rousseau's Tiger
- 34 A Woman Peeling Apples
- 35 Autograph
- 36 Lost At Sea
- 37 Spring Equinox, North London
- 38 Quince, Orange, Pear
- 39 Hostage to Fortune
- 40 Reflected Object
- 41 War Story
- 42 Old Woodworking Tools
- 43 Tools of the Trade
- 44 Foliage

- 45 Our Woman in Havana
- 46 Doing Time in the Movies
- 47 Seasonal Scenes
- 48 Day of the Dead
- 49 A Nun's Last Confession
- 50 Pied Piper
- 51 An Existential Reading of Newton
- 52 Another Country
- 53 Up the Creek
- 54 Silver Fox
- 55 Message from a Bottle
- 56 Postcard from Dracula
- 57 The View from Pine Ridge, South Dakota
- 58 In Regent's Park
- 59 Mr Quercus Speaks his Mind
- 60 Double Exposure
- 61 Tequila
- 62 Woke Up This Morning
- 63 Bless My Soul
- 64 The 'if' in California
- 65 Arc
- 66 On First Seeing the Bay Area's Homeless
- 67 Jetlag

Alphabet

Auchendrane was our pit-stop on the way to
Ballantrae where we would spend the summer in a
Caravan my grandparents owned; my mum and
Dad would turn up 2/3rds of the way through,
Easing out of work & routine, then Nana & Willie
Folded up their holiday for the drive back to Glasgow,
Glad the weather had been kind and there were no
Horror stories to impart about mishaps this year, no
Injuries to complicate things, no accidents playing with
John the son of the farmer who owned the site, or
Kenneth his younger brother, who would chase
Lambs on the farmland up the hill, until evening
Mealtime called a halt to the day's adventures, and
Nighttime in the Ayrshire countryside would define
Ordinary over & over until the holidays ended and
Parting for another season or another year defined the
Quality of whatever relationships had been formed, the
Reverse of our normal lives in Glasgow, a foreign place in
Summer until just before the school term started, then
Tractors became something glimpsed on television or seen
Under a shop lights as models, and I wouldn't see the
Vauxhall the farmer drove with one arm across the
Wheel until eventually next year's Easter holiday
Xxxx'd its way across my grandmother's calendar
Yet every year except one till I was 15, we took photos;
Zorro swords, bikes, swimsuits, an alphabet of memories.

Kraut

Hitch-hiking is a good test of character,
once you know you can't get home that evening,
healthier than public school or military service.
I was lucky; I did my road stint in the early 70s,
saw plenty of western Europe, never made it
to India, nowhere exotic, not even Ireland,
nearly stayed in Germany, though later
I preferred Dutch freaks to German hippies.

German drivers always had lots of money,
and precise *Voice Of America* English.
I enjoyed good luck with Mercedes drivers,
some of them doubtless served in the SS
or learned to drive in the Afrika Korps,
but they were polite and played Mozart tapes.
The one I remember best drove me briskly
through fifty miles of world-famous industry
and talked about his experiences as a POW.
He was in a Camp in the Scottish borders.

His radio gave us *Udo Lindenberg Und Das PanikOrchestra's*
electric violin instead of Bach: sacrilege, no?
He asked about Die Ibrox Panik Katastrophe.
Yes, 66 died; no I wasn't there, saw it on the News.
He told me Honduras & El Salvador went to war
after a football match, showed me a stamp
his brother sent from Brazil; Pele's 1000th goal.

He left me with lunch and a last question;
'One thing I never understood you know;
why you Britischers called us Krauts –
when I was a guest of Mr. Churchill
I never ate so much kraut in my life.'

Weather Reports

Blizzards in Scotland. A939 Cock Bridge to Tomintoul closed.
Every year we bet on the likely date of Radio 2's
winter mantra, thankful we lived a hundred-odd
miles south of this pagan weather, smirking at
the notion of sharing Moscow's latitude.

We were temperate, only political interests
in common, remembering it was Chicago
which took its weather from Moscow,
its iron-frame architecture from Glasgow,
its music from Kerry or Mississippi.

That climate shocked Muddy Waters
& Willie Dixon into rewiring the Blues;
as Lenin might have prophesised to Engels'
US pen-pal Florence Kelley-Wischnewetzky,
Rhythm & Blues = Chicago + Electricity.

A music that might have shocked Engels
as much as the meat-packing plants,
steelworks and South Side tenements
which powered it up,
                              flipping the coin

on the Country & Western energising
the shop on Hope Street which sold
Western gear to Glasgow's cowboys,
all the saddles, leather chaps, stetsons,
boots & spurs a hombre could desire.

We loved every music America offered,
even Bluegrass, our own tunes in disguise,
leaving strathspeys & reels to folkies
quoting Satchmo: *all music is folk music,*
all of us trapped in the blizzard of history.

Born to be wild

400 watts of white noise filling
the *Spanish Lounge*, Bellshill;
doesn't sound much these days,
but the drummer had to ballast
his bass drums with 56lb weights.

An audience of Blue Angels,
Glasgow's outlaw biker clan,
hair flying, beards wagging;
the exact attitude of Jews
before the Wailing Wall.

All drinks one price,
point to what you wanted;
sign language an art form
learnt quickly when all sounds
had equivalent value.

At closing time the Angels
would march from the bar,
cock a leg over their choppers
in unison and roar off in a blur
of leather & *heavy metal thunder*.

When I was in Glasgow last year
I could barely recognise Maryhill,
couldn't find the *Tramcar Vaults;*
who would I phone up 25 years on
to learn where the Angels are now?

The Reddest Shoes

Mine were gold-laced crimson Fiorucci, matching
Kate's scarlet studbright strappy stilettos.
Paris awarded those in 78 for mere money.
Our chorus *The Angels Wanna Wear My Red Shoes*,
Moira Shearer something for our parents.
We were skinny & speedy in leather jackets,
knew every band with a guestlist worth gracing.
Our scene fell apart too soon, playing out
the Country & Western song of your choice.
Six months later I stepped under a taxi.

Kate joined a Welsh commune; I went nowhere.
I think the 80s happened to someone else.
Now I'm a fat Chartered Librarian in Barnet.
Kate lives in Clapham, works in Oxford St.
One day I was browsing the new releases
in Concerto Records; fairground mirror time.
In Nutters Meatfree Zone I learned that
the 80s passed Kate by in Wales then Brighton,
she doesn't like Classical or the punters,
feels cheated music is only a job. My career?

'Chartered - you sound like a City accountant.'
I examine my brogues, her brown Hush Puppies,
finger the diamond of scar tattooed on my cheek
by her Parisian instep before we broke up.
I found that shoe's partner behind the wardrobe,
had it sealed in a fluid-filled perspex box,
pass it off as Damien Hirst or Antony Serrano.
After our *St. Linda Special* we tally the log of
friends dead of drugs, AIDS or missing in action,
don't kiss, walk off in different directions.

Buttons

Used as currency in childhood card games,
shipped to America with blankets, axes,
coloured glass, used as means of exchange
with the Five Nations; Manhattan traded
to Peter Minuit for 60 guilders in trinkets,
the best real estate deal in history.
Brooklyn also sold to the Dutch West India Co,
trading arm of the Dutch Reformed Church.
Wall St. dividing the haves from the have-nots.

The laws native Sachems spoke resemble
Brehon law, no concept of private ownership,
land held in trust for the whole tribe
by elected chieftains; some lived in towns,
some lived *much like the wild Irish.*

Any English village's children could have
bought America with their playthings;
who can say if the Nations knew or cared
what deal they were doing, Turtle Island
big enough to house the 'Coat-Wearing People'.

Tribes treated worse than children,
yet they bartered fish, beaver, tobacco,
took up arms in the 'Cut-Throats' wars,
mixed these up with their own wars,
killed by smallpox blankets & firewater.

They lost everything on the wager
that they were dealing with a people
who would treat them honourably;
now they run casinos on tribal land,
make the odds, hand out wampum,
take the Yanqui dollar, a fair exchange.

Cloths from Rajasthan

These are the colours of heat.
Earth baked to hot hard brick.
Coriander, cinnamon, saffron,
rice & sweetmeats passed from
hand to hand on a silver platter,
left hand an aid to conversation,
right hand the only utensil.

Gauzy shimmer. Dust. Camel dung
collected for fuel & moustache wax.
Camel races; sword-width moustaches.
Bets on everything in sight.
Men judged by their moustaches
and riding skills, valued in camels,
looking like the Punjabi Sikhs
who drive Glasgow's buses.

Music & dancing after sunset,
their instruments mediaeval
to our ears; dholak, kamaicha,
satara, morchang, santoor;
too wild for any orchestra.

The Thar Desert rides a red turban
towards the North-West Frontier,
Baghdad of the Caliphs only a camel
charge away, and if the Silk Road
runs again because of oil in Baku
these men will start in Lahore.

Whatever happens can be blamed
on the Mujahadeen or the CIA.
In the meantime, moustaches
are waxed, camels are raced.

Coming Back to Clear up

Next time round I want to be a goat,
eat whatever I want without guilt;
if I return far enough in the future
I can be an android or cyborg goat.

That way I can clean up whatever
mountain I happen to be posted to,
tin cans, abandoned implements & all;
as part organic I can mate as well.

No fun being a goat without the sex.
Not that I feel guilty about my life
contributing to the mountain of trash
burying the Himalayas in separate instalments.

I'm not a bloody tourist, I pay enough
in fees to visit this part of the world.
I live to climb, enjoy the Peak Experience
(& every other bad pun devised over

Imported beer in the *Up & Down Disco*).
Round up the hippies in Kathmandu,
put them to work clearing up the mess;
work as meditation, I like that.

I'm sure they would too, given a chance.
What would the hippies come back as?
Mostly sheep, yaks, the occasional tiger,
their own younger selves given the choice.

Reincarnation

I woke up to find myself hugging a rock.
I don't remember falling asleep, passing out,
or even dying; what did I do to deserve this?

Almost everything was different except the rock.
Rocks are reassuringly reliable almost everywhere.
I couldn't tell if I was on a beach or a desert.

With no horizon and not many other features,
it was hard to tell if this was a small rock and
I was a normal frog, or frogs were house-size here.

Yes, I appeared to be a large lemon-yellow frog
according to the ripply mirror of the pool I crept down to.
It tasted ok, nothing attacked me, I walked away.

Yes, it's hard to let go of those old assumptions.
But soon I wanted insects to eat, water lily leaves
to jump from, and other frogs to mate with.

So I set off across the granular – yes, sand, thank you –
up a slope, down another slope into this valley,
which is either full of dwarf plants or I am huge.

You are the only other sentient being I have met.
You appear to be a car-size red spider. I hope
we can be friends, allies, or just good neighbours.

What do you mean, 'Don't feel like a spider?'
Do you think we're hallucinating at a party?
Trust me, you won't wake up in your old life.

Naughty Boy

The blackest bag over my head.
I am sure I will not choke.
I like coal dust and insecticide
up my nose and down my throat.

I love dancing with rat after rat,
spreading the walls with squeaks,
the scrabble of coal under our feet
mimics a skeleton shaking rainsticks.

Red eyes signal rats or tarantulas.
Moonlight creeps under the door
forever, it will not cut off my toes
as it swallows the cellar floor.

I do not want a pillow,
I do not miss my Teddy;
if I recite every prayer I know
I can make morning come quickly.

When Daddy unbolts the door
I will not flinch when he hoses
me with tobacco fumes and beer.
He will open the door. He will.

Holiday Joke

These two feminists from Birmingham
Fatima & Leila decide to go on holiday.
'I fancy somewhere foreign' says Fatima.
'Yeah somewhere exotic – how about Wales?'

So they're cycling through Shropshire
and it's getting towards lunchtime.
They don't like the look of the villages,
the villages don't like the look of them.

Market Day in the next decent-size town.
'There must be a veggie restaurant here.'
When they march into the Masonic Arms
a long roomful of farmers falls silent.

'Is it something I said or what, Fatima?'
'Nah they just can't understand your accent.'
'Check the graffiti – PAKEY GOE HOAM.'
Ploughmans Lunch twice, table near the door.

Farmer Jones shoots past singing *Sospan Fach*.
Back of the Land-Rover – his sons & two sheep.
'Look at that Leila – that's disgusting that is.'
'I know – I really hate them arranged marriages.'

Thinking Your Way Round Clichés

A stone in a river
is a stone in a river.
Seeing it   really *seeing* it
will not gain you enlightenment.
Neither will it hold you back
if you do not see it.

It might break your ankle
if you stumble over it
after not having seen it.
Sitting in the river
thinking *Now* I see the stone
is not enlightenment either.

Following the river
to a lake with a heron
is not enlightenment.
Comparing the heron to a priest
has been done before by poets.
Rivers of ink   Gaelic to Chinese.

Knowing this comparison
has been made before
will not gain you enlightenment
nor will it make you a better poet.
The heron is made of limestone.
It is a memorial to a priest.

Jacob and the Angel
Genesis Ch.32, v.24-32

There is always a test.
This time it was a wrestling match.
Not in a fairground booth
not in the public arena
not even in a tavern
but in my own garden.
At night all through
the blackest night I can remember.

I know three different wrestling styles.
She or he knew these and more.
Yes, I said he or she.
Couldn't I tell man from woman
even in the dark? This was both
or neither but not hermaphrodite.
I met one of those one,
I know the differences.

Our grappling was fast as water
or slow as rocks; a furious patience
with no room for error or fumble.
We taught each other new moves
while clouds danced across the sky
and foxes & cats went about their business,
appraising our slick configurations
as if this happened every night.

The wings were a problem,
breaking my grip time after time,
catching on the ground.
Dawn found us face to face
skin to skin to skin.
In the end I demanded
a blessing in exchange for release.
I was given a new name, *Israel*.

All We Are Saying

I once saw a flock of Hare Krishnas
shuffling their mantra up Grafton St.
performing their own stereotypes.
It can't just be the shaven heads,
the outfits, the sandals, the drums
they manage to beat slightly out of time.

Don't they ever rehearse or do they
practice that to win the sympathy vote?
Is something added to their brown rice,
are they subjected to psychic surgery,
or do they just reject anyone who doesn't
fit the profile, no matter how sincere
their commitment to Krishna Consciousness?
As Freud used to remind his disciples,
If you look like one, you are one.

How would Hare Krishnas fare in Belfast,
would Ian Paisley harangue them from corners,
would every Orange Lodge they passed
square up & play *The Sash* on their flutes,
parade their Lambeg drum to demonstrate
a proper marching rhythm; would Sinn Fein
see a threat if they conga'd up the Falls Rd,
send out a Republican Flute Band to show
again how flutes destroy rational thought?

If enough Hare Krishnas colonised Belfast
and chanted loud enough & long enough,
would Adams, Hume, Trimble, Paisley,
forget about who & why they think they are,
long enough to *Give Peace A Chance*?
What's wrong with being governed by zombies?

Attachments

Irish nurses do the best urban myths.
Re-arrange your life to suit their shift patterns,
massage their back, cook whatever they desire
while they sluice off the blood & assorted
bodily fluids, then take them out dancing,
to the Safari Park, or down Holloway Rd
for some Shamrock & Western, and let them
unpack their kitbag of patients peculiarities
that could still get someone from another clan
accused of witchcraft in some countries.

After you've heard this a few times, Bacardi
& Guinness are flowing free, what you want
to hear is the log of their adventures in Casualty,
things too weird for *Understanding Nursing Care*
or too squalid for Sister to joke about in lectures;
the uses of household appliances not covered
by the warranty, their scorn for people cruising
Soho or surfing eBay when any Plumbers' Merchant
stocks everything they need for a loving relationship,
exploring their sexuality, or learning discipline.

They like to watch *real men* play Gaelic football,
confide what people do with Hoover attachments,
or anything that comes to hand and hits the spot.
If you ask nicely, if you are very, very good,
they might share the secret of their Xmas Quiz -
who arrived in Casualty with what during the year.
Prizes in each category are always something to eat,
drink, or share with a friend. Mentioning *Operation
Spanner* sets them off on true tales about referees'
& politicians' personal lives in Kerry and Mayo.

Manchester's Big Mistake

Is being Manchester; too Irish, too Jewish,
too bloody Northern for Brian Sewell's taste.
We can't have a Holocaust Museum here
just because a few Asiatics escaped some
pogrom or other. Who remembers Armenia
in 1915 he drawls; we do, Brian, we do.
We don't have the luxury of aestheticising
experience, of pretending that only socially
conscious art is 'political', or forgetting Wilde
wrote *The Soul of Man under Socialism*.

Picasso's all right nailed to the Prado wall,
Brecht's all right entombed in the Olivier,
Irish music's all right cordoned off on Radio 2,
the history of Cottonopolis can accommodate
Hard Times or Engels without bothering too
much about the likes of Mary & Lizzie Burns
whose labour power produced the profits,
whose class consciousness educated Engels
whose money gave Marx leisure to do his work;
he should have been a watchmaker or tailor,

or Talmudic scholar, kept his place & lost his dreams.
Manchester is full of people whose grandparents
found out too late that Salford was not Brooklyn,
and this would have to be home. Cheated?
Of course not; Manchester isn't *England*,
I mean it's not the Home Counties, Brian.
But if you ignore the weather and the food,
strange looking people with peculiar accents,
it's preferable to Vilna, Belfast or Armenia,
anywhere else people hate you for being different.

Refugee Status

The sky flashes pink/green/pink/grey
through the larch trees lattice; occupying
the plain below us, is a town my parents
cannot name. Nana would if she could speak;
she knows the place, its local delicacies,
the local dances, what rogues the traders are,
which edge of the border jigsaw we fit on.
Every day we have learned the same lesson
about strokes, wheelchairs, and old women.
My sister died in these woods two days ago.

This town has a large square, a town hall,
a campanile, no church that we can see.
There will be banks, pawnbrokers, phones,
fax, perhaps a bribeable clerk or official
who will let us board a bus or train quietly.
This morning Mama found our lost heirlooms
in Nana's soiled underclothes. Two weeks ago
selling these things could have flown us out.
Now we would have to take our chances here.
First we have to steer Nana down this slope.

Uncle Paul would not have gotten this far;
he sought sanctuary in the Hospice opposite
the unmarked building where he was grilled
by men in matching leather coats, beaten &
broken, dumped in an alley, pissed on by dogs,
left as crow meat for professing his faith in public.
The ten-year-old robbers who took his shoes
& wallet shouted this news up to our window.
We packed one bag each before the Official Visit.
Now we will see how far our faith takes us.

Exhibit

There was this whitewashed wall.
It had clusters of head-height holes
at regular intervals. At first I thought
it was an Art Gallery, then I noticed
patches of sun & shadow on cobblestones.
Ah, I thought, public art, municipal art,
this is a civilised country after all,
where taxpayers flourish credit cards over
something domestic scale & affordable.

Look again, the whitewash is new,
dark splotches of something previous
showing through, not enough detail
for a mural, perhaps something in
the Jackson Pollock line, defaced or
censored by concerned local citizens.
Perhaps someone's art got ruined,
and they need my cousin's number,
he specialises in municipal lawsuits.

Have I seen this wall before?
No, I haven't. (Of course I have,
I inspected this courtyard each Friday,
gave demonstrations with my father's Mauser.
Morale & tradition march together.)

What happened behind the green door?
Did I give an after-dinner speech, *Torture:
the most fun you can have in a uniform*?
Everything Papa taught me clear in my head,
his voice guiding me now; *Admit nothing,
Ignore the camera; Do not recognise this Court*.
I say this photograph is a forgery.

In My Dreams

I am being pursued through Mexico City
by a taxi full of priests dressed in black.
I look back, their suits are identical & stylish,
they sport dark glasses & matching haircuts.
They sit bolt upright, look neither to left
or right, do not smile, indulge in small talk,
or gesture at anything their taxi encounters.
They appear to be exactly the same height.
I am not used to teams of stylish priests
sitting in a taxi giving orders to the driver,
following me. These gents are obviously not
seminary boys from Maynooth or Stonyhurst,
I doubt they have family in Mayo or Donegal.
In fact I can't imagine them as altar boys
even though there nothing Calvinist,
Methodist, or even secular about them.
Their vocation fits them as though tailor-made,
their faces are smooth and pale, their soft
hands unmarked by cigarettes or work.
It doesn't matter what else has happened
in the dream, at some point their taxi
appears behind me, turning the corner
at the far end of the street, just close
enough for me to register the black suits,
their bland expressions, the lean over
to their driver, his nod & gear change.
Occasionally, they stop the taxi and get out,
look around, confer, and get back in.
If I can see the black case they carry
through the open door, they are too close.

Rodin's *Left Hand*

Is reaching for a cello's darkest note,
is black & shiny as a burn victim.
Death is reflected in its glossy finish,
the erased roadmap of the smooth palm,
the missing fingerprints the Sûreté
could not read in 1885, the absent nails
Rodin would have loaded with clay
or garden soil if he had bothered
to make such a concession to realism.

The wrist is lumpy like a snake
which has just eaten well, and has
energy to spare travelling along
its length, the movement upward
to test the air, flourish its grace note
before spiralling down to silence.
His signature is stamped across
the wrist, as if to ward off Alzheimer's;
every time the hand is raised it says
this is who I am, this is what I do.

Or maybe the hand mimes a double bass,
anticipating the arrival of jazz in Paris,
the Minstrel Shows, Dixieland Bands
bringing Congo Square to Montmartre;
what the Burghers of Calais are keening
as they raise their hands in despair is
'No Adolphe, a thousand times No,
your saxophone is not for military bands,
it is the voice of the new century;
you wouldn't believe the sounds haunting us,
we dream of Charles Mingus and Charlie Parker.'

The Artist's Mother

My Andrej was a good boy.
The mask he wore for you
was just that; all thought
there was nothing behind it,
like he was a *robota*.

Well he was, he worked
at his movies, his art,
but underneath all of
Manhattan varnish, he was
still my son, still good
Catholic, came to visit
his mother, regular.

Oh, you didn't know that,
you think New York is
whole world, outside is
wilderness. Well, I tell you,
my father, God rest him,
came from Ruthenia, from
real forest with real wolves.

So my Andrej painted your
America for you, Monroe,
Presley, those soup cans.
Real life – eating soup
in front of a television.

I taught him his Catechism.
He was altar boy till
he was 14 then chose Art.
I wanted a priest in family,
I did not stand in his way.

Art Gallery Weather

Outside, the sun mimics
the all-seeing eye
in Van Gogh's painting.
These chopped down
sunflowers in a jar,
these irises not waving
but drowning, the crows
hurled across the sky
above bent cypresses
and boat-fearing corn
are not symbols of
anything, do not stand
for anything except
the state of Van Gogh's
nerves after too much
absinthe or spending
all his food money
on tubes of paint.
When he cut his ear off
it was not a gesture,
when he shot himself
it was not a cry for help,
nor did he hear voices.
Was he mad not to
paint like Fantin-Latour
or follow Gaugin to Tahiti?
Unlike the struggling artists
in *La Bohème* he lacked
the temperament to treat
the whole thing as a game.

Rousseau's Tiger

I am the Invisible Tiger.
Nobody ever sees me till
I want them to. Too late.
Ha ha. Jolly fellow I am,
such a fine laugh I have.

Look closer. You don't
like my laugh, don't like
my teeth? Oh I say,
bad show, bad form.
Where were you raised?

If I'm not perfect in form,
I'd like to know who is.
Not you, didn't even know
I was here. What's wrong
with your eyes & ears?

You don't belong here,
but you're staying for
dinner; nothing formal
you understand, no need
for the old penguin suit.

I say, could you run
just a little bit, what?
Make you taste better.
I prefer vegetarians.
I hope you don't drink.

Now then, don't do that.
I said don't! Now then,
dinner, if you could just,
that's better, now this
will hurt I'm afraid.

A Woman Peeling Apples

after Pieter De Hooch

Thank you Nel, put the peel into the bucket,
the pigs must eat too if we are to eat well
over the winter. Yes I know you like them,
they are your friends, but they are only pigs.
Where do you think your breakfast came from?
No the butcher is not a bad man to kill animals,
that is the bargain; we give him the pigs,
he gives us bacon, pies, sausages, pork.

Papa will be home next week, God willing,
and he wants to see our larder hung with
good things to eat, so that we will not starve.
You remember the Cornellison boys; yes,
to the Orphanage they went, their parents
were not thrifty, nor God-fearing, nor clean,
so God took their parents, and now look.
No we will not take them in, we have
enough to do minding our own affairs.

Soon I will teach you your letters Nel,
then you will see how hard we work
to make a living for ourselves; do you think
this basket, that bowl, the coal in the fire
that cooks our dinner, was got for nothing?
How do you think you are not in rags
like those children you saw yesterday?

Your Papa is a clever man with a good eye
for what the merchants will give good prices.
Now hand me the next apple, then go wash
your hands. No you cannot go out in the yard.
Yes Papa will be home soon, yes he will have
presents, no he will not bring you a monkey.

Reincarnation

I woke up to find myself hugging a rock.
I don't remember falling asleep, passing out,
or even dying; what did I do to deserve this?

Almost everything was different except the rock.
Rocks are reassuringly reliable almost everywhere.
I couldn't tell if I was on a beach or a desert.

With no horizon and not many other features,
it was hard to tell if this was a small rock and
I was a normal frog, or frogs were house-size here.

Yes, I appeared to be a large lemon-yellow frog
according to the ripply mirror of the pool I crept down to.
It tasted ok, nothing attacked me, I walked away.

Yes, it's hard to let go of those old assumptions.
But soon I wanted insects to eat, water lily leaves
to jump from, and other frogs to mate with.

So I set off across the granular – yes, sand, thank you –
up a slope, down another slope into this valley,
which is either full of dwarf plants or I am huge.

You are the only other sentient being I have met.
You appear to be a car-size red spider. I hope
we can be friends, allies, or just good neighbours.

What do you mean, 'Don't feel like a spider?
Do you think we're hallucinating at a party?
Trust me, you won't wake up in your old life.

Naughty Boy

The blackest bag over my head.
I am sure I will not choke.
I like coal dust and insecticide
up my nose and down my throat.

I love dancing with rat after rat,
spreading the walls with squeaks,
the scrabble of coal under our feet
mimics a skeleton shaking rainsticks.

Red eyes signal rats or tarantulas.
Moonlight creeps under the door
forever, it will not cut off my toes
as it swallows the cellar floor.

I do not want a pillow,
I do not miss my Teddy;
if I recite every prayer I know
I can make morning come quickly.

When Daddy unbolts the door
I will not flinch when he hoses
me with tobacco fumes and beer.
He will open the door. He will.

Autograph

*'As a teenager, I went to poetry readings like pop concerts:
I heard Norma MacCaig, Peter Porter, Adrian Mitchell
when I was 15, 16.'*
(Carol Ann Duffy, *Guardian Weekend*, 25/9/99)

Norma MacCaig spoke Gaelic very loud and very fast.
She wrote very quietly and very slowly in English
and Gaelic, in invisible ink, sang the Metrical Psalms.

For many years a printer's error made Norma
the only published Gaelic woman poet in Scotland.
Edinburgh's literary elite found this amusing.

On learning she wasn't Iain Crichton Smith's muse,
they decided she was a lesbian & spat in her sherry.
Exiled from Edinburgh, airbrushed out of photographs.

By the time women her granddaughter's age
were writing & publishing in either tongue,
Norma was silent in her writing and in real life.

She was a schoolteacher 40 years in Wester Ross,
taught generations of girls to love both languages,
sent them out into the world with her blessing.

In 1982 she produced her best creative work;
Visa application accepted, she spent two days
revising her autograph: Miss Normanon MacCaig.

Train to Glasgow, taxi to Wylie & Lochhead,
four Laura Ashleys, six pairs of shoes,
an Astrakhan coat, a Kathleen Ferrier box-set.

Norma appeared in Court once, and print twice more –
the *Daily Record* and an obituary in the *West Highland
Free Press*. Neither mentioned her poetry.

Lost at Sea

Holidays provide the acceptable face of difference,
like Radio Landlady from the b&b kitchen:
an iceberg 183 miles long by 22 miles wide –
half the size of Wales – is adrift in the Ross Sea;
on Papua New Guinea the typical family unit
features husband, wife, & 2.4 anthropologists;
death is the punctuation for the life we lead.

Time to play 'Exploit Me I'm A Tourist',
buy postcards, local delicacies, a guidebook,
inspect the Castle's Jacobite memorabilia,
then follow the harbour from yachts to trawlers.
Two big boats chug in under a cloud of gulls.

I watch the crew on the *Stella Maris*
doing sailorly things till a dark-haired lad
looks up and sings out in the local dialect
'Oh I say old chap, do run along now.'
One crew climbs the iron ladder, stands silent,
watches the other ascend then walk towards
the row of cars parked on the hotel forecourt.
One man carries a lifejacket and a duffelbag.

That evening the guidebook sent me to a pub
noted for the quality of its traditional music.
A chair by the fire stayed empty in a full bar.
A fisherman laid his fiddlecase on the musicians' table,
smacked down the late edition of the local paper,
folded open at LOCAL MAN LOST AT SEA.
After a glass of Glenmorangie, he struck up
two sets of reels, a strathspey, then a slow air.
The other musicians looked up; 'A new tune?'
'Aye, ye can call it "The Empty Chair" if ye like.'

Spring Equinox, North London

Camden Council has declared Spring.
The outdoor pools will open to the public
regardless of temperature, or whether
the good people of Hampstead, Highgate,
Kentish Town, Gospel Oak, Camden Town,
are ready and willing to take the plunge.

Soon, the perverts & peepers will creep
from their lairs to the Women's Pool,
the Men's Rights nutter will try and join
those PagenAnerchystLezbyan frolics,
anglers will strangle swans with plastic & lead,
dogs will gobble up last night's pavement pizza.

Blindness will not hinder two swimmers
from lunging in head-first for forty lengths,
this room will echo to the sound of rain
that might cleanse the air of winter or might
give the People's Republic an expensive
soaking in a weak sulphuric acid solution.

Alternative Therapists will offer clients
and anyone scanning *Time Out* or library leaflets
a safari to improbably remote Welsh teepees for
Spiritual Healing & Shamanic Drumming Weekends
whose suggested donations would make a lawyer
blench and consider a change of career and name.

Anyone whose biggest adventure since the Scouts
or Guides was an Arvon course gets their chance
to learn what the natural world does all day, what
Lenny Bruce meant by *Every day people are staying
away from Church and going back to God;* go home,
get in touch with the *genius loci* of Waterlow Park.

Quince, Orange, Pear

An Elizabethan still life,
in the manner of the Dutch,
something to balance those
pheasants, hares or trout hung
on the other side of the room.
Everything seasonal & valued
whether common or shipped.
Quince the last relic of our
mediaeval diet, jelly or tart,
cooked with chicken, alternate
with honey at table before
sugar or molasses sweetened
the Triangular Trade.
Oranges & sherry the only
welcome gifts from Spain,
shipped in October in time
for Christmas, to partner
apples on the board,
marking off mid-winter.
No more fresh fruit in
the hand until the early
orchards or south-facing
walls in sheltered gardens
offer up their prizes.
Pears climb into baskets,
form into orderly pyramids,
run their juice down chins
in order of precedence,
say to everyone
I am Summer, eat me.

Hostage to Fortune

What fruits would he have tasted or seen
at home in Raphoe Castle or Derry City,
before he was taken to London to entertain
Elizabeth's Court as 'the Queen's O'Dogherty'?

Apples certainly, pears, plums, raspberries,
anything native to the North, maybe oranges
shipped with wines from Madeira and Jerez,
those second-best seasonal gifts from Spain.

Did they think Sir Cahir green or unseasoned
to be impressed by quinces, forswear Gaelic
tastes, grow pliant enough to be fashioned
into an English gentleman who would speak

the Queen's tongue & promote the Queen's
peace in his corner of Ulster to his cousins?

Reflected Object

It is reflected in several panes of glass, consecutively,
occasionally doubling then winking out of view.
I can see it for as long as the glass holds it.
If I look away, does it cease to exist, or will it
arc its way across the real world for as long
as anyone choosing to watch keeps it in view?

Where do reflections go when the glass stops?
Do they have a secret life beyond the borders
of our notice, where we cease to exist for them
and their world has its own laws, customs, history,
which we can imagine only if they choose
to imagine ours, a one for one trade-off ?

If a swimmer meets his reflection as he dives in,
which world does he enter and on whose terms?
Does that reflection enter our world, take his place
and go about his business on its own terms?
What have our doppelgängers done in our name
that we would refuse, deny, or say 'I wish I had'?

If there is a version of us entered into some other
place, space, or world, what have we been doing there?
If you can't dive into the same river twice, is that
truly another life, or are our selves mindless as fish,
not knowing if they have done anything before,
no memory of anything previous to give them a self?

If seeing what we truly want to see is an act
of sympathetic magic, who makes the choice,
and is it the same on both sides of the mirror?

War Story

Red signals blinked across hazy fields.
Mother was hard at work harrowing
the soil, clucking the horses onwards.
These days, there were no tractors about,
anything mechanical commandeered
for the War Effort. She tried to ignore
the body laid out neatly at the margin
of the field, its hands folded quietly
on the breast, as if enjoying a nap
after lunchtime beer & sandwiches.

His shirt's poppy-red stain was redder
than the flowers on Mother's pinafore.
She wanted to shake some answers from
surly men in gaberdine & trilbys sneering
farm work wasn't War Work, demanding
the truth while a cart was readied to remove
the body to the Station and her nephews,
the only lads of working age here, hustled
away; she wanted to know what *intern* meant,
where did they imagine their food came from?

Mother knew they were poking & prying
in her home & every cottage for two miles,
wondered if some local lass was mixed up
in this business, looked up, saw the biggest,
blackest, thundercloud primed for action,
thought about tarpaulins, coats, scarves,
evidence about to be washed away, how
none of this would put food on anyone's table.
Never mind this spy or whatever he was;
she wanted her menfolk back here now.

Old Woodworking Tools

Their names and forms are mediaeval.
Boys became men after seven years usage.
Now they lie jumbled on trays in Camden Lock
or shops in Upper St. with post-modern prices.

Paint has erased itself from handles,
wooden shafts have Old Masterly patinas,
more forlorn than ever they were in attics.
Who cares if they are rusty or incomplete?

They are objects soaking up disposable income.
In action they shed oil, shavings, blood.
They adorn shelves in houses whose original
owners treated their handlers as tradesmen.

Even in homes which have been restored
to the specifications in *House & Garden*
these tools speak a foreign language
scorned by cowboy builders' Estuary English.

Once, a careless hand picking up these tools
mimed the arcana of demarcation disputes.
Now they are stripped of all mystery & craft;
electricity pours four men's work into one handle.

Knowing the right name, its possible use,
will impress dinner parties, might even turn
a two minute demo into a weekend project.
By Sunday evening they are merely objects again.

Tools of the Trade

Almost anything you think of has other uses.
Car radiators in home distilling, household
appliances for personal fulfilment, hairspray
as artists' fixative; *Blue Peter* showed the way.

But what really excites our interest is torture.
Water, electrics, hoods, dogs; been there, done that?
If Security sign you up, who supplies your kit;
buddies, discreet shops, catalogues, e.tailers?

Is it possible to show too much initiative?
How much would you be allowed to enjoy
your work before you were transferred
to a Black Squad or the Invisible Academy?

If you came in one Monday morning with a tool
they'd never thought of before, would they fetch
up test material from the cells or strap *you* down?
Could you free yourself using only your tongue?

If your boss produced a banjo one afternoon
how much trouble would you think you were in?
If he said *The Anti-Christ supports animal rights
& the environment* would you know who to arrest?

If a man called Shakespeare a *swivel-eyed shirt-lifter*
would you take him to the alley for questioning,
ask yourself what were you doing in that sort of bar,
or take him away for a serious code-breaking session?

Foliage

How many shades of green are there?
The song says forty, an important number
for connoisseurs, a seasonal, tempting
sort of number, taking two people to count.

DIY Stores offer dozens I'd refuse as decor,
Pantone's colour chart sports thousands.
This common or garden selection before me
shows my suburban eye savoury handfuls.

Thin stems, thick stems, blades, laces, clovers,
each leaf with proper use & lore, good or ill;
some smell so familiar I must know their names,
might have thrown them into pasta or stews.

The dominant smell is an open cupboard,
a spilled lid, a steamy saucepan waiting
for the magic touch of tarragon or oregano,
when an ordinary evening becomes an occasion.

I understand the importance of pestle & mortar,
why a walk through the woods between meals
is healthy, why real gardeners carry clasp knives,
why musicians' shelves feature oregano & nutmeg.

Art Pepper recorded these herbs for Discovery Jazz,
a hint to hipsters; if Mary-Jane was on holiday
down Mexico way, a trip to the grocery store
or a rummage round the kitchen did the trick.

Our Woman in Havana

Never met Graham Greene,
read his novels for O-level,
has mostly forgotten the plots
but still remembers Pinkie in
Brighton Rock and his cut-throat
razor, something she has never
seen in real life. The clothes
the characters wore, assuming
the film with a baby-faced
Richard Attenborough got it
right, resemble the zoot suits
from her favourite musical
era, and would probably be
popular in Havana, which
seems to be frozen in 1956.
Only in Havana's streets
could you find a pig tethered
to a vintage 1950s Cadillac.
The pig could outrun the car,
the petrol crisis might outlive it,
even after Fidel *goes to meet Marx*.
The building they are parked
outside could camouflage
the pig, the one next door
matches the Cadillac's seats.
In a hotel down the street
a group of elderly gentlemen
are playing tunes they learnt
before Castro started smoking.
English tourists are tasting Salsa.

Doing Time in the Movies

If you achieve *human interest* in real life
Hollywood has the right to steal your story,
package it, soundtrack it, dump whatever
they can't use on the cutting-room floor,
then sell you all over the Western world.

You can't copyright your life, unless you get
your autobiography or first novel into print,
but Hollywood can & will sue you for fraud
if they write your life first. Will you be given
a sight of the script or veto over the star?

How would you feel after Meryl Streep
or Mel Gibson impersonated you on screen,
then in every shop people nudged & stared,
told their kids that you weren't really *you*?
Would you be disappointed with yourself?

Would you feel obliged to have a makeover
or would you adopt your screen look then
join an Agency to impersonate yourself,
and get paid for life to open supermarkets?
Would you demand the lead in any sequel?

How would you enjoy being a Celebrity,
always in the tabloids as your doppelgänger,
with a lifestyle paid for as long as you played
their game, a career being not-quite-yourself,
or would you do your 15 minutes then retire?

Seasonal Scenes

It is always Summer in Spencer's Cookham.
Either he saw it that way all year round,
sensibly spent his winters somewhere else,
or sat indoors before any available fire;
'Pissarro painted south London in winter
so I can follow my own inclinations here,
Cookham a state of mind as much as south London,
and if it snows anywhere in the Bible, quote me
chapter & verse, or rain except for Noah's Flood.'
Life in the Church of Me has one season.

His Cookham is fecund, verdant, unbuttoned,
his radiant characters sport long hair & robes
as if rehearsing for the 60s, miming middle-class
bohemians of the sort who live all around me,
people who can't remember the 60s because they
lived that dream, the sort who sent their kids off
to have adventures in the summer while they lived
life with a capital L, knowing that nothing bad
could ever happen with the Woodcraft Folk,
and Famous Five escapades were not plausible.

Often these families decamped to Morocco
or maybe their kids never went to school,
the whole concept of 'holidays' meaningless,
their family merging with other families
as the Me Generation went communitarian,
everyone got stoned, *Straw Dogs* a bad trip,
& they discovered the necessity, if not the virtues,
of hard work, sharing still a great ideal, providing
there was something to share, and somehow winter
seemed to last most of the year in the real world.

Day of the Dead

after Stanley Spencer; *The Resurrection, Cookham,* 1924

If this were Mexico, mariachi trumpets
would welcome the lurid skeletons
to dance for their friends and families,
cavort round the zocalo, two-step
down the main street and into a cantina
for tequila and chocolate-sauced chicken.

But this is Berkshire, a milder and more
decorous awakening, no music to hand
unless the languid male nude centre stage
is looking off towards a Salvation Army band
blaring out *Onward Christian Soldiers,*
wishing them to march into the next village,

so that he and his wife, the only other nude
in sight, could step out of their modesty,
borrow some clothes from the vicar's wife,
go about their business, while other people
awaken in stages, alone or in family groups;
no-one pays any attention to the African family

who might wonder *where & how are we,*
before remembering their last lives, asking,
have our prayers to our gods failed,
are we truly children of this pale Christ,
who must be powerful indeed if these dead
arise whole, clothed, unblemished, refreshed;

all except one man who sleeps on,
unconcerned by all this stir & bustle,
as if his time has not yet come, or perhaps
this *is* his time; he has the luxury of sleeping in
or sleeping on, knowing that when he wakes,
they will be ready to receive him.

A Nun's Last Confession

My name is Aschenputtel.
I was born in another country
a long time ago, in a fatherless
house occupied by my Aunts.
They were such grand, busy
persons, there was no room
for me; I lived where I worked,
in the kitchen. They hardly
saw me yet I felt their hand
whenever anything went wrong.

My father was a sea-trader.
I overheard them arguing
how to spend the legacy
he left for my education.
I had no mother, no name,
not a word from my Aunts.
A week before my 16th birthday
I had a visitor while my Aunts
were fumbling silks & satins.
She gifted me a promise.

Of course they went to the Ball.
They failed the Prince's test,
sharing the Court's shock when
he knelt to his prize at last.
They did not attend our wedding.
My greatest achievement was not
healthy sons, tax reforms, the Hospital,
but burning his Castle to the moat
after he debauched his pageboy
then sired one bastard too many.

Pied Piper

He didn't make us do anything.
We didn't follow his flute, his purse,
or his promises, just our own desires.

When he got rid of the rats, once & for all,
or at least until next Spring, we didn't care.
We could have told him, if he'd asked,

that he wouldn't get a penny piece
from the Town council of Hamelin. We knew
our Elders, we were seen & not heard.

But when the rats left, so did the cats.
What use are slingshots with no targets?
I mean the rats, most of us liked cats.

We asked for more pocket money, were beaten.
We thought about following the cats to farms,
or bigger towns, or just living in the woods.

Our Elders made it very clear their rules
governed our lives, in their dull little town.
Then one Spring day, the Piper came back.

We met him at the West Gate before dawn.
Our knapsacks were packed, yet our Elders
say he bewitched us, led us under Koppelberg.

As if we were more easily led than rats.
I ask you. Who do you think wrote down
the story, passed it around the countryside?

An Existential Reading of Newton

The Universal Clockmaker hates His work.
He does not know why He does this work,
who created Him, or if He created Himself
before or at the same time as everything else.

He does not know if He is the only Clockmaker
or how He would find them or what would
have happened if one day another knocked
on His door and said *Brother, Friend, Daddy.*

What if there is another Way of doing, being,
making; who or which is right or wrong,
does Someone else stand behind them,
is He an unknowing co-worker or competitor?

He sets His work in motion, moves on,
does not look back or meddle, though once
He drowned one whose noise offended Him.
It started up again, He walked away.

Sometimes He thinks there are other Universes,
but cannot remember if He made them,
or whose dream He might be part of,
what happens if He wakes up and says *NO.*

Or has He spent Eternity meditating
on all of the possible consequences
of His one original decision or action,
His almighty hand frozen in mid-gesture?

Another Country

I am watching *Whistle Down The Wind*
in Ilford Town Hall; we are translated
to an ideal 1950s. I am a foreigner here
among the good people of Essex.

Where do the 'Home Counties' stop?
In Glasgow we never knew ourselves
provincial, but Second City of Empire.
Tonight it is foggy enough for the real 50s.

Mods vs. Rockers in Margate, Whitsun 64;
first sign of aliens, then incense, bells & ragas.
Bring back conscription: El Alamein veterans
stranded between space cadets & the Patels.

Ilford's 70s went disco-daft then Punk.
In the 80s they voted for themselves.
My Afghan hat does not belong here,
sneer Wayne & Sharon: *stupid old hippie*.

A station poster paraphrases James Dean
for a West End *Whistle* translated to Dixie.
We are all nostalgic for different things;
I might feel more at home in this other South

as long as the rifle slung across his shoulders
is purely a style gesture, not a statement
of fundamental belief in *different* as threat
and your hat declares which side you're on.

Up the Creek

Crocodiles are not scared of helicopters.
Forget all those lovely films with herds
of zebras, rhinos or species of antelope
you can't spell, wheeling across the savannah
as the ground shadow of a chopper advances
inexorably towards them, or crocodiles
slipping off sandbanks into turgid rivers
as David Attenborough's canoe putters past.
Crocodiles' walnut-sized brain tells them
the whole world is their *AllYouCanEat* buffet.

He should try Disney World for a week sometime.
After 5 days in Miami where we met four Don
Johnsons, drank Cuba Libres in a bar with marlin
on the walls & Jimmy Buffet on the jukebox,
learnt 40 ways to insult Castro in Spanish,
met some Gooners craving Courage & kebabs,
and fell in love with a Brazilian transsexual,
we hired a van and drove into the Everglades,
home to alligators, snapping turtles, American
crocodiles, and 140,000 Burmese pythons.

We parked at the Marina Store in Flamingo,
loaded an airboat with rum & key lime pie.
Our pilot laughed when we hit something,
pointed out the cottonmouths in the water.
Then the engine died. We are surrounded
by wildlife. We discuss *Live And Let Die,*
Roger Moore dancing across a row of crocs,
the proper use of one paddle, where's the rifle,
response time for 911 calls. If *Crocodylus acutus*
is the endangered species here, I'm Captain Hook.

Silver Fox

My wife observes my beard is going silver.
She says this makes me look distinguished,
a family codeword like *refined* or *educated*.
I'm not sure I like being *distinguished,*
even though I've turned a corner this year.

Watching Andy lose his King of the Garden title
then go thin before he died was bad enough,
the surprise, his fur changing colour in patches.
Now *Compendium* has retired the spirit of 1968.
Neither of these why I'm wearing black today.

Someone who thinks fat is healthy confides
I'm looking well: *you used to look so frail.*
501's and Doc Martens tag me as style victim;
Radio 4 is my daytime listening, Radio 2
sounds good after dark with a bottle of port.

Soon the suit I bought for degree ceremonies,
weddings, bar mitzvahs, court appearances,
will be used more & more for funerals of people
my own age or younger, or replaced by one that
fits me and enhances my new silver fox status.

Parts of me stay 12, 22, 30, whenever I first heard
the Stones, Little Feat, Gregory Isaacs, Art Pepper.
My music refuses to grow old gracefully, still
believes in changing the world or just being cool.
This year's signature music is Bach's *Cello Suites*.

Of course I'm consumed by the usual vanities,
body hair relocates as if hormones are kicking in
again; today I found a patch of hair on my back.
Dirty Old Man syndrome or born-again werewolf?
There were always words for people like me.

Message from a Bottle

The label is a work of art in its own right,
Francis Bacon shrunk, discreet & manageable,
the smears, daubs & drips rehearsing a history
of its original purchaser, or whoever got it
as hand-me-down, retrieved it from a garden
or skip, took it to Art College or Evening Class,
or palmed it from the bathroom, rinsed out
its residue and installed it in their workshop.

Calamine lotion, turpentine, linseed oil;
whatever it held, nowadays any shop
in walking distance won't recognise these,
never mind being able to point you to a shelf
where you might reach down a bottle freckled
with plastery dust, with a price tag so faded
it might be pre-decimal, or so implausible
Mrs. Patel wonders if she can sell it to you.

This ghost of the *goodwill* which swallowed
their savings after escaping Uganda, glued
to the rear top shelf by sheer recalcitrance,
might be part of the original stock, a remnant
of Crouch End's exclusive past as a village
which had an Opera House, then a municipal
concert hall, and still has cricket pitches.

Milk & mail arrived first thing in the morning.
Sawdust in the Butchers, carbolic soap in kitchens,
beeswax in the parlour; all nice and public.
Let's not forget the catsmeat, tripe, trusses,
the back bedroom with its shelf of bottles
the doctor took 5/- to say *might do the trick,*
or might end up discarded, leaking vague fluids.

Postcard from Dracula

It never rains on Planet Postcard;
wouldn't be good for the tourist trade.
I ghost-wrote the original *Rough Planet*
Guide, so many places I've lost count.
Every time I take the long sleep
my memories are collaged. I think
I invented False Memory Syndrome.
I am my own unreliable witness.

That's why I collect postcards,
one of the few Victorian inventions
I approve of. Museums make me
queasy, bringing on flashbacks,
but their shops sell me back parts
of my past, provided I possess
the right currency in my pocket.

Sometimes I forget that gold
is no longer universally good,
except in some mediaeval desert
I sincerely hope I never visit again.
I saw *Doctor Who* once, in 1965,
and recognised the Doctor's plight.
That's how my coffin malfunctions
when my resting place is disturbed,
just dumps me anywhere, anywhen.

Just look at this, *Whitby Harbour,*
I remember this a hundred years ago,
I might have written a novel about it,
It was a dark and stormy night etc.
I have written most of my lives,
will enjoy my royalties in perpetuity.

The View from Pine Ridge, South Dakota

a response to Bill Woodrow

Out here on the High Plains
is the world's junkyard.
Once you've bought it
you can't take it back.
Once you've used it
it won't go away.
Some of it will rot,
some of it will rust,
some of it will cut
our children open.
Some of it will choke
the birds & animals.
Why do you think we care?
Will you pay us to make sculpture?
If you think any of this
is Art, take it away.
Does your neighbourhood
look like this? If not,
why not? Someone
like you made this stuff,
someone like you
sold this stuff to us.
You have everything else
in your Museums,
why not have these
authentic artefacts as well.
They're just as genuine
as canoes, tomahawks,
wigwams, head-dresses.
Promise me you'll take it all.

In Regent's Park

I am ballasted with mud and gravel.
If I grace your table you will not notice this,
although if you eat me in some Tuscan trattoria,
I hope the shotgun pellets choke you.

I am the drunken oboe behind your picnic.
Soon your son will guess the note once too often
and your wife will remember her Uncle Jack
in Canada and wish to wield his gun again.

If he approaches too close I will present
2 dozen mouldy buns and you will think
for a moment your son is calling his favourite bear,
or that someone has disgraced themselves again.

I am water, air, the glaze of slime on your trousers
which recalls the Tang Dynasty pottery you saw
in the British Museum, or the flying horse in Gerrard St.
which bent your Access Card out of shape.

I am the paddle-boat your son wants to take home.
He has offered to dig me a pond in the garden,
thinks I am here to be his home video, does not
understand *migrate,* that he may not see me again.

Mr Quercus Speaks His Mind

When I was young I was struck by lightning.
several of my companions were also hit.
At first I welcomed this; more space,
more light, more wind to wake us up.
But gradually I realised that more wind
could knock me about, loosen my footing,
perhaps bring me low before my time.

And I found I missed those nearby voices.
Some of the others were so badly hurt
they were taken away; when I was very
young I was told terrible stories about
that sort of thing – I thought they were
fables, could not credit the use to which
we might be put. Now I know better.

Now I am old and creaky, wishing
I lived somewhere warm and dry.
I have never really minded the birds,
but the squirrels irritate more & more,
and I find that I positively hate humans.
More chatter, more damage, more often

Perhaps there have always been too many,
always wanting too much from the world,
or they're not using each other up fast enough.
I suspect they are also living longer.
Could lightning strike enough of them down
to change things or just slow the process?

Thinking like this is not good for me.
I'm sure they have poisoned the rain.
More and more I find myself meditating
on what happens next, on my next life.

Double Exposure

'All we wanna talk about is Readers' Wives'
(Dave Edmunds)

Film rolled in sporting random aliases,
wage slips wore different logos every week.
I worked with all these women dressed
in Indian national costume, grey anorak
& brown cardigans, shaking their heads,
'My God aren't the English strange.'

They copied the kinky stuff to take home.
They told me they could read *The Sun*
but they couldn't read the *Kama Sutra*
in Sanskrit or anything in Hindi or Gujarati.
They would stroll up fanning their faces,
'What you think of this?'; 'You try this at home?'

I sent extras of the Sharons & Tracys
shot on some suburban terrace afternoon,
curtains drawn, lights on, to *Readers' Wives*
complete with the punter's name & address.
I hope they enjoyed adorning garage walls
or being pasted in toupee'd Sales Reps' toilets.

One day two blokes charged into Reception
waving the mag & a pickaxe handle each.
The Management grovelled, paid out,
interviewed us in English, Hindi & Gujarati.
All three shifts got letters: unpaid suspension,
then total sackings if nobody owned up.

Suddenly I became *Studentboy* – 'It must be him.'
Three different Mrs. Patels recalled me saying
'This is how you turn film into memories.'
I skipped past a thicket of hockey sticks.
I haven't set foot in Willesden in 30 years,
still feel nervous in Brent Cross or Ikea.

Tequila

Flavoured our tongues with Mexico,
shots of Jose Quervo with salt & lemon,
in the *Hope and Anchor* or *Dingwalls,*
falling in love with the bar staff, who taught
us to love Tequila Sunrise, put the Eagles
on the jukebox, then The Champs, *Tequila*!
fuelled up for Ian Dury or Dr. Feelgood
in the *Hope*'s cellar, then *Dingwalls* later.

We downed Red Stripe stagefront, where
Muddy Waters is the King of Mississippi,
all he needs is that crown Queen Ida wore
when she brought her Zydeco circus to town,
& suddenly Eric Clapton is up on stage
and ready to jam with Muddy, who turns,
stares, lays down his guitar & stomps off,
slamming the dressing-room door hard.

Clapton looks like an art student again
but the band don't care, striking up a tempo
that makes Clapton sweat out some of his
best blues for years, 15 minutes of glory
for this audience, and tequila is downed,
Red Stripes are raised, some wag shouts
Slowhand to cheers all round, then too soon,
he is off stage, and through the stage door.

Muddy Waters emerges, kicks his chair aside,
grasps the mike stand, roars out the intro
to 'Mannish Boy' then the band kick in.
This is the moment we have waited for
since buying *Muddy Waters at Newport*
aged 12, and after the encores are over
we will storm the bar & order more tequila
till we are comatose and ready for taxis.

Woke Up This Morning

The first thing he notices on waking
is a concertina of leather trousers
suggesting Jim Morrison is alive & well
and got him howling drunk last night.
Soon he is spitting blood in the bathroom,
guessing what his tongue is coated with,
thinking coffee yes, toast yes, fry-up *neurgh,*
what adventures did he have to make
his legs this rubbery, or has he just been
practicing the lotus position in his sleep?

Listening to the News on 5 Live is a mistake.
Opening the blinds proves the clock right,
he has 15 minutes to prepare for work,
this is Monday, he is on Counter Duty
in the Library today, and it's raining.
His search for the Paul Smith suit he thinks
he was wearing is cut short by a snow-dusted
voice from the kitchen which wants a beer,
declaims *In Swahili there is no word for coral,*
sings what might be a Randy Newman number,

Ah'm a Rear Admiral in the Confederate Navy,
confides Elvis is a tour guide in Père Lachaise.
This man is his own leather-clad monument,
tanned & glinting, ready to kickstart the day.
The words Library and Work set him off;
Art is the cargo cult of the bourgeoisie.
Our librarian admires those leather strides,
supposes the other pair must be his,
thinks his last definite memory is answering
'Sure Jim,' to 'Can you play keyboards?'

Bless My Soul

Margot announces it is the Buddha's birthday.
I suppose she means the historical Buddha,
Siddharta Gautama, called Shakymuni,
because if there are Buddhas all around us,
there must be birthday parties all around us,
one for every Buddha, or perhaps they invite
each other to their parties, concerts or ceilidhs,
like Elvis impersonators who invite friends,
family and workmates to their talent contests
to witness their repertoire of gesture, posture & words.

Perhaps every Elvis impersonator is a Buddha
and the Big Mac is the attachment that hinders
Enlightenment, or perhaps if they are Enlightened,
they can scoff Big Macs without spiritual harm.
Elvis impersonators will take over the world,
an Elvis will be the next President, the next Pope,
Elvis will be spotted in Cuba, Albania, North Korea,
Elvis will be the next Dalai Lama, and McDonald's
won't be able to build Burger Heaven fast enough.
50 million Elvis impersonators can't be wrong.

If you haven't made the pilgrimage to Graceland,
you don't dare tell your friends or neighbours,
who won't invite you to bowling or BBQ's again.
Of course you can't always recognise an Elvis,
just as you can't recognise a Buddha till it's too late
to ask your one burning life-changing question;
anyone who looks like an Elvis, walks like an Elvis,
talks like an Elvis, is probably a Pat Boone devotee,
hasn't played any Elvis since 1972, can't remember
his birthday or where they were when he died.

The 'if' in California

became my beacon at 14, when I was
a resident alien at home; I still want to get
there before they declare Independence,
raise the Bear Flag high, proclaim their
indifference to events on the other side
of the Rockies. Of course Sacramento
might not stay capital long, before
a Civil War breaks out between North
and South, LA secedes, Mexico wants
everything up to say, Monterey back,
or they apply to join the new Republic.
What would Oregon & Washington do
then, secede from the Union in sympathy,
form a Pacific Federation or deploy
the Oregon National Guard to save
themselves from being Californicated?
Could San Francisco defend itself against
San Diego if things turned mediaeval?
Would the Bay Area Homintern perform
well in khaki or would they still be bitching
about the accessories as they were interned
on Alcatraz? I can imagine pledging
allegiance to the flag of the 7th richest
country in the world, with its own Navy
at San Diego, Edwards Air Force Base,
Twentynine Palms Marine Corps Base,
Berkeley to provide internal opposition,
wineries, the cuisine, civilised weather,
Hollywood to make the myths. New York
is history here as long as there's an if.

Arc

Canadians can outtalk Texans on size;
moose will win that argument every time,
big hat no cattle gets you sent to Calgary.
Flying to San Francisco from London
seemed to happen mostly in Canadian
airspace, hour after hour overflying
the sort of Arctic waste the Mounties
always got their man in; there really
was no hiding place, or at least none
unclaimed by wolves or hibernating bears.

The pilot pointed out salient features
as if we might need to remember these
if the plane crashed and we survived.
Places I had heard of materialised,
arranged carelessly on either side of
the 49th parallel's ideological construct;
Mt. Hozomeen, Desolation, Terror,
proved suitably awesome & desolate
but Jack Kerouac danced into my dream
waving his wine jug shouting *Go! Go!*

I had looked forward to seeing Denver,
keen to match *Dynasty*'s credits to reality,
as the plane cruised over the Rockies,
but our world is a multi-dimensional book,
& now, following the Earth's curvature,
I was flying west into a new morning,
the arc over Iceland, Greenland, Canada
shadows the Viking route to Vinland
where everything seemed possible
and still does to travellers heading West.

On First Seeing the Bay Area's Homeless

I count at least 200 in one downtown block,
notice far more women than in London,
and that the obviously mad or addicted
are a small minority among this minority
where 'people of color' are the majority.

The *San Francisco Bay Guardian* claims
14,000 live in their cars, on friends' floors,
in Golden Gate Park, or hustling on the street,
where it must become easier not to see them,
as if they have no right to stand in the light.

Do you give at random or just stroll on
until someone's spiel gets your attention,
like the Jewish gas money panhandler,
or the Haight St. hipster who sold me
a poetry mag featuring Jack Micheline?

At Pier 39, the Human Jukebox sings me
Otis Redding's 'Dock of the Bay'; later
the *Street Sheet* seller down on Hallidie Plaza
has a well-honed spiel and regular buyers,
is confident enough to flirt with women.

This is America after all, he is making
the most of his opportunities, and could
make a good guess at which BART station
in Contra Costa County they call home.
He turns his back on the drug dealing.

Over in Oakland I meet hundreds more.
'Please give me some money so my son can eat'
one man's pitch outside *Yoshi's Jazz Club,*
now I will never hear 'Dock of the Bay'
without seeing the boy on his shoulder.

Jetlag

I lie in bed convinced I am in two places at once,
then start to hear strange noises in the house,
not the central heating, fridge, cistern or radio.

I want lunch in *Mario's Bohemian Cigar Store,*
what I have is a cold kitchen, an empty fridge,
baggage, a rucksack of t-shirts, cds & books.

Today I am on automatic pilot, doing everything
with deliberate care; for once I empathise with men
who simplify their lives with routine or drink.

Time to test Radio 2's notion of *warm & bright.*
Soon I find myself wandering round Crouch End
confused by currency, the local beer, and traffic.

I never experienced San Francisco's legendary fog,
does it wrap the senses in harmless cotton wool,
or act like LA's smog, a toxic blanket over the head?

Glasgow had ghostly pea-soupers in the fifties,
obliterating the third dimension till we walked into
something or someone, or came to a kerb & halted.

Was anyone foolhardy enough to drive through it,
did they obey the traffic lights if they appeared,
or were people pragmatic enough to stay at home?

How do San Franciscans cope with this irruption
of the natural world into their playground, does it
bring out their generosity when tourists make fools

of themselves, or do local opportunists lurk to catch
anyone who hasn't realised what the rules are here,
or like me, is just confused by the changing light?